THE KITE RUNNER

by
Khaled Hosseini

Teacher Guide

Written by
Pat Watson

Note

The 2004 Riverhead Books paperback edition of the novel, © 2003 by TKR Publications, LLC, was used to prepare this guide. The page references may be different in other editions. Novel ISBN: 1-59448-000-1

Please note: This novel deals with sensitive, mature issues. Parts may contain profanity, sexual references, and/or descriptions of violence. Please assess the appropriateness of this book for the age level and maturity of your students prior to reading and discussing it with them.

ISBN 978-1-60539-048-2

Copyright infringement is a violation of Federal Law.

© 2008 by Novel Units, Inc., Bulverde, Texas. All rights reserved. No part of this publication may be reproduced, translated, stored in a retrieval system, or transmitted in any way or by any means (electronic, mechanical, photocopying, recording, or otherwise) without prior written permission from ECS Learning Systems, Inc.

Photocopying of student worksheets by a classroom teacher at a non-profit school who has purchased this publication for his/her own class is permissible. Reproduction of any part of this publication for an entire school or for a school system, by for-profit institutions and tutoring centers, or for commercial sale is strictly prohibited.

Novel Units is a registered trademark of ECS Learning Systems, Inc.
Printed in the United States of America.

To order, contact your local school supply store, or—
Novel Units, Inc.
P.O. Box 97
Bulverde, TX 78163-0097

Web site: novelunits.com

Table of Contents

Summary 3

About the Author 3

Characters 4

Background Information 5

Initiating Activities 6

Eight Sections 7
    Each section contains: Summary, Vocabulary,
    Discussion Questions, and Supplementary Activities

Post-reading Discussion Questions 25

Post-reading Extension Activities 28

Assessment 29

Scoring Rubric 37

Glossary 38

Skills and Strategies

Thinking
Analysis, compare/contrast, brainstorming, inferring

Comprehension
Cause/effect, summarizing, predicting, conflict/resolution, decision-making

Literary Elements
Theme, metaphor, simile, symbolism, foreshadowing, irony, characterization, setting, genre, tone, style

Writing
Journal, poetry, script, review, monologue, sequel, riddle

Vocabulary
Target words, definitions, application, connotation, denotation

Listening/Speaking
Discussion, performance, reports

Across the Curriculum
Music—appropriate selections, ballad; Art—collage, montage, poster; Current Events—research, newspaper/magazine articles

Genre: fiction

Setting: Afghanistan; Pakistan; California, United States; 1963–2002

Themes: sacrifice/suffering, rejection, discrimination, guilt/redemption, friendship, loyalty, gratitude, humility

Conflict: person vs. person, person vs. self, person vs. society

Tone: serious, sincere, realistic

Mood: dark yet also wistful

Style: first-person narrative

Date of First Publication: 2003

Summary

The narrator, Amir, recounts and reflects on his childhood as the privileged son of a wealthy Pashtun businessman and his friendship with Hassan, the poor, illiterate son of the family's Hazara servant. Although Hassan is Amir's servant, the two boys spend countless hours playing together, and Hassan is Amir's kite runner during the traditional kite-fighting tournament. During the tournament in the winter of 1975, Amir betrays Hassan when he fails to intervene and prevent his beating and rape by the cruel Assef. Amir then accuses Hassan of stealing in order to drive him and his father away from Kabul. For the next 26 years, he struggles with guilt over his disloyalty to Hassan, whom he eventually discovers is his half-brother. Amir seeks to redeem himself by rescuing Hassan's orphaned son, Sohrab, from Afghanistan and giving him a new life in the United States.

About the Author

Personal: Khaled Hosseini was born in Kabul, Afghanistan in 1965, the oldest of five children. His father was a diplomat with the Afghan Foreign Ministry, and his mother was a teacher at a large Kabul high school. The family moved to Tehran, Iran in the early 1970s but returned to Kabul in 1973. The family relocated to Paris, France in 1976. Their plans to return to Kabul were thwarted by the Soviet Union's invasion of Afghanistan. The Hosseini family was granted political asylum in the United States in 1980 and moved to San Jose, California. Khaled Hosseini lives in California with his wife, Roya, and their two children. In 2006 he was honored to be named a United States goodwill envoy to the United Nations Refugee Agency (UNHCR).

Education/Career: In 1984 Hosseini graduated from Independence High School in San Jose. He earned a bachelor's degree in biology from Santa Clara University in 1988 and entered the University of California-San Diego's School of Medicine, where in 1993 he earned his Medical Degree. After completing his residency at Cedars-Sinai Hospital in Los Angeles, he was a practicing internist from 1996 until 2004. He began writing his first novel, *The Kite Runner*, in 2001. Upon its release in 2003, it became an international bestseller and was eventually published in 48 countries. The novel was named the Barnes and Noble Discover Great New Writers Selection, a *San Francisco Chronicle* Best Book of the Year, an *Entertainment Weekly* Top Ten Fiction Pick of the Year, an American Library Association Notable Book, and was the recipient of The American Place Theatre's Literature to Life Award. His second novel, *A Thousand Splendid Suns*, was published in 2007 and became a #1 national bestseller.

Characters

Amir: narrator and protagonist of the story; a privileged child of the Pashtun upper class in Kabul, Afghanistan who often treats his servant and best friend, Hassan, with contempt; flees Afghanistan with his father after the Soviet invasion and starts a new life in California; is plagued by the guilt he feels for betraying Hassan

Hassan: caring, gentle son of Ali; serves as both servant and friend to Amir; devout Muslim; approaches life with a loving and forgiving attitude; loyal to Amir his whole life; marries Farzana and fathers Sohrab; murdered by the Taliban despite his unquestioning respect for Afghanistan's class divisions

Baba: Amir and (secretly) Hassan's father; well-liked and admired in the Afghan community, for which he does many good and charitable works; Amir's idol; remains aloof to Amir during his childhood; wracked with guilt for dishonoring Ali; leaves behind his life as a wealthy businessman in Afghanistan and takes a menial job in the United States

Ali: loyal Hazara servant who is part of Baba's family for 40 years and is like a brother to him; loving father to Hassan; ridiculed by Pashtun boys due to his appearance; killed by a land mine

Rahim Khan: Baba's best friend and business partner; encourages Amir and understands his struggle to gain his father's approval; knows about Amir's betrayal of Hassan and offers him a chance to be good again by getting Hassan's son out of Afghanistan

Assef: antagonist; sociopathic, cruel Pashtun boy who bullies other boys in Kabul, including Amir and Hassan; beats and rapes Hassan; admires and wants to emulate Hitler; becomes a high-ranking Talib in Afghanistan, using his power to prey on others, especially Hazaras

Sohrab: Hassan's orphaned son whom Assef takes for his sexual perversion; tries to commit suicide when existing trauma and Amir's unintentional betrayal are too much for him to bear; eventually shows promise of recovery after Amir brings him to the United States

Soraya: Amir's wife; also suffers from a "sin" in her past, i.e., running away with a man when she was 18; kind and compassionate; unable to have a child of her own and gladly accepts Sohrab

Sanaubar: Hassan's beautiful but unscrupulous mother who deserted him five days after he was born; taken in and cared for by Hassan when she returns years later

Sofia Akrami: Amir's lovely, educated mother who died giving birth to him

Mahmood and Tanya: Assef's parents; intimidated by their son and cater to his wishes

General Iqbal Taheri: Soraya's father; worked for the Ministry of Defense; Baba's friend who respects Amir; proud, mercurial, and controlling; suffers from migraines

Jamila Taheri: Soraya's mother; feels unappreciated by the general; has a beautiful voice but is forbidden to sing by the general; adores Amir, especially since he is willing to listen to her troubles

Farid: driver who takes Amir into Afghanistan in search of Sohrab; initially has no empathy for Amir but comes to respect him; takes care of Sohrab and provides support as Amir recovers from severe injuries

Wahid: Farid's brother; gives Amir a place to stay when he returns to Afghanistan and feeds Amir though his family has little food; calls Amir "a true Afghan"

Zaman: runs the orphanage where Sohrab is placed after his parents' deaths; periodically sells a child to keep his orphanage running

Raymond Andrews: seemingly uncaring official at the American embassy in Islamabad

Omar Faisal: affable lawyer who tries to find a way for Amir to take Sohrab to the United States

Kaka Sharif: Soraya's uncle; works for INS; instrumental in getting a humanitarian visa for Sohrab

Background Information

The following information will enhance the students' understanding of the novel.

1. Time line of key dates in Afghanistan's history: July 17, 1973—Daoud Khan, in a bloodless coup, deposed King Zahir Shah's regime and became president of the Republic of Afghanistan; 1979–1980—Soviet Union invaded Afghanistan and installed a puppet government, which sparked opposition by freedom fighters known as *mujahideen*; 1988–1989—Soviet troops withdrew; 1992—The *mujahideen* removed Mohammad Najibullah's Soviet-backed government; 1993—Rival factions chose Burhanuddin Rabbani to be the new president, and Afghanistan descended into lawlessness; 1996—The Taliban, led by Mullah Muhammad Omar, seized control of Kabul, began enforcing a harsh interpretation of Islamic law, exiled President Rabbani, and offered protection to Osama bin Laden; 1999—The Taliban took control of Mazar-i-Sharif, and many Shi'a, especially Hazaras, were killed; September 11, 2001—Terrorists, under bin Laden's leadership, attacked the United States; December 2001—The United States and its allies helped Afghan rebels force the Taliban from power; 2002—Hamid Karzai became president of Afghanistan, and the U.S. placed about 12,000 troops in Afghanistan.
Source: http://www.infoplease.com/spot/taliban-time.html (active at time of publication)

2. Muslims/Islam religion: founded by the Prophet Mohammed in the seventh century; two branches now exist—the Sunni (about 90% of the Muslim world) and the Shi'a. The groups diverged in 632 due to disagreement over who should lead the Muslim community following Mohammed's death. Violent opposition between the two factions continues.

3. Hazaras: Afghan ethnic group considered to be lower class; speak Farsi and are mostly Shi'a Muslims

4. Pashtuns: Afghan ethnic group considered to be upper class; speak Pashto and are mostly Sunni Muslims

5. Urdus and Tajiks: other ethnic groups in Afghanistan

6. Farsi: language spoken primarily in Iran, Afghanistan, Tajikistan, and Pakistan

7. Taliban, a.k.a. Students of Islamic Knowledge Movement: one of the *mujahideen* groups formed during the Soviet occupation of Afghanistan; ruled the country from 1996 until 2001, during which they instituted rampant public executions and other extreme punishments, banned "frivolous" activities, banned women from working outside the home, and forbade girls to go to school

8. Northern Alliance: Afghan rebel group that controlled Kabul between 1992 and 1996

 It is especially important to note the mature subject matter of *The Kite Runner*. The novel contains profanity, references to sexual misconduct (such as promiscuity), offensive (slang) terminology, as well as a graphic scene of child rape. This rape is the basis of the building action in the novel and is referenced many times throughout. Please also be aware of the following: Due to the ongoing tensions in the Middle East (both within the area and with the United States), the subject matter of *The Kite Runner* may affect each student differently. Please be prepared to deal with the individual thoughts and emotions that will surface during the study of this novel. Please carefully consider your particular community and group of students prior to reading and discussing *The Kite Runner* with your class.

Initiating Activities

1. Preview the novel. As a class, discuss what the title suggests about the novel. Note the illustration on the cover, read aloud the synopsis and the blurbs on the back cover, and read some of the comments in the introductory section. Have students make predictions about the novel.

2. Brainstorm with students about their knowledge of the history of Afghanistan from the 1980s to the present. Have available recent newspaper or magazine articles about the continuing strife in this country.

3. Place the word "guilt" on an overhead transparency. Brainstorm with students about the possible connotations and denotations of the word, the results of guilt, and how guilt can be alleviated.

4. Write the following quote from British statesman and philosopher Edmund Burke on an overhead transparency: "All that is required for evil to prevail is for good men to do nothing." Discuss with students what they think this means and how it may relate to *The Kite Runner*.

5. Play 15–20 minutes of the 2007 film adaptation of the novel, which is available on DVD (*The Kite Runner*: 2 hours, 2 minutes; DreamWorks studio, distributed by Paramount Vantage; rated PG-13 for strong thematic material, violence, and profanity). Then ask students to write a paragraph explaining what they think will happen to Amir and Hassan.

Chapters One–Four

The narrator, Amir, reflects on the significance of a phone call he received from a close family friend, Rahim Khan, a year ago. Amir begins recounting his childhood in Afghanistan and explaining the complex relationship between himself, his father, Baba, and their servants, Ali and Hassan. Though Hassan is Amir's best friend, matters of ethnicity, class, and religion threaten to drive a wedge between the two boys, and Amir often feels he must compete with Hassan for Baba's affection.

Vocabulary

- unatoned
- cleft lip
- ethnic
- Mongoloid
- mullah
- aficionados
- impeccable
- imbecile
- hone
- irony

Discussion Questions

1. Analyze the metaphorical statement, "…the past claws its way out" (p. 1). How does it relate to the information the narrator, Amir, reveals in Chapter One? What might Rahim Khan's statement mean? *(The past is like a living entity that Amir cannot escape. He tried to bury it, but after 26 years it has resurfaced. Amir visualizes the moment when something happened in the winter of 1975 that continues to haunt him and has shaped much of his life. Rahim Khan's phone call from Pakistan represents the resurfacing of Amir's sins. Rahim's statement, "There is a way to be good again" [p. 2], implies that Amir now has a chance to confront and atone for his sins.)*

2. Compare/contrast Amir and Hassan, noting their backgrounds, how each boy interacts with his father, and the circumstances surrounding their births. *(Amir is a Pashtun [upper class]; Hassan is a Hazara [lower class]. Amir's father, Baba, is affluent; Hassan's father, Ali, is a servant. Amir lives in the most beautiful house in his district of Kabul; Hassan lives in a little hut. Amir gets a good education; Hassan is illiterate. Amir's mother died during his birth; Hassan's mother deserted him when he was five days old. Amir feels rejection from his father, who rarely has time for him; Hassan is his father's greatest joy. Both boys nursed at the breast of the same Hazara woman, leading Ali to believe they have a kinship that nothing can break. Amir's first word is "Baba," indicating his idolization of his father; Hassan's is "Amir," indicating the high regard in which Hassan holds Amir.)*

3. Discuss the origins of the ongoing conflict between Pashtuns and Hazaras. What effect might this have on Amir and Hassan's relationship? *(Conflict between the two ethnic groups stems from their religious backgrounds. Pashtuns are Sunni Muslims, and Hazaras are Shi'a [Shiite] Muslims. During the nineteenth century, the Pashtuns persecuted and oppressed the Hazaras when they tried to rise against them. Pashtuns killed many Hazaras, drove them from their lands, burned their homes, and sold their women. Hazaras have Mongoloid features and are often called derogatory names. Pashtuns, who comprise the affluent, educated class in Afghanistan, generally consider themselves superior to Hazaras, who are characteristically poor and illiterate.)*

4. How does Amir feel about Baba? Examine information about Baba, and discuss how Amir and Baba's differences affect their relationship. *(Amir is awed by Baba's strength and the admiration others have for him. Indicative of his strength and physical appearance, he is known in Kabul as "Mr. Hurricane." His building of an orphanage with his own money reveals his benevolence. His business ventures with Rahim Khan allow him to become one of the richest merchants in Kabul. He married Sofia Akrami, one of the most beautiful, educated women in Kabul and a descendant of the royal family. Amir knows his father is disappointed because Amir is not athletic and does not even enjoy watching sports. Baba is ashamed of Amir because he never fights*

back when others mistreat him, and he is impatient when Amir fails to understand what he is trying to teach him. Amir believes his father hates him because he caused his mother's death. He escapes his father's aloofness by reading voraciously.)

5. What does Baba say is the only sin? Explain his theory and whether Amir is able to understand it. *(He believes theft is the only sin and that every other sin is a variation of theft. He rationalizes his theory by pointing out that murder steals the life of the victim and his family, lying steals someone's right to the truth, and cheating steals the right to fairness. Amir understands this theory because a thief stabbed Baba's father and killed him, thus robbing Baba of a father.)*

6. Examine Baba and Ali's relationship. How is Amir and Hassan's relationship similar to theirs? What impact do their ethnic backgrounds have on these relationships? *(Baba's father adopted Ali when he was five years old after he was orphaned by the tragic deaths of his parents. He and Baba grew up together, just as Amir and Hassan grow up together a generation later. Baba coerced Ali into carrying out his mischievous ideas, just as Amir coerces Hassan into carrying out his mischievous ideas. Though both relationships are characterized by a brotherly closeness, neither Baba nor Amir thinks of his Hazara companion as a friend because of their different ethnic backgrounds; i.e., nothing can transcend the history of the Pashtuns and Hazaras. Amir and Hassan play together constantly, but during the school year, Hassan performs all the duties of a servant and Amir attends school. Amir and Hassan spend long hours on a hill close to Baba's property where Amir reads to Hassan and carves their names on a pomegranate tree there: "Amir and Hassan, the sultans of Kabul" [p. 27]. However, Amir, who realizes how intelligent Hassan is, cruelly teases him at times, especially in word "games" that expose his ignorance. Amir enjoys Hassan's loyalty and adulation [of which Amir sometimes takes advantage], but when Hassan's insight reveals a fault in his first story, Amir resents him. The class dynamic in Afghanistan establishes an unhealthy dynamic in Hassan and Amir's friendship, Hassan as the humble giver and Amir as the haughty taker.)*

7. Discuss the significance of Hassan's favorite book, the *Shahnamah*. *(The epic intrigues Hassan, and he never tires of hearing Amir read it aloud. Amir's and Hassan's favorite story is "Rostam and Sohrab," a tale in which the warrior Rostam mortally wounds his nemesis, Sohrab, and discovers he has killed his own son. Amir associates this story of a son's search for a father's love and the father's stubbornness with his and Baba's relationship. Just as Rostam kills his son, Amir believes his father has a secret desire to kill him.)*

8. Assess the role Rahim Khan plays in Amir's early life. *(Throughout Amir's childhood, Rahim seems to understand Amir better than Baba and encourages Amir in his endeavors. Rahim tries to get Baba to accept Amir as he is and stop trying to mold him into a duplicate of himself. When Baba seems distant [as when he shows no interest in Amir's first story], Rahim steps up as a stable and supportive father figure for Amir.)*

9. **Prediction:** To what is Rahim Khan referring when he offers Amir a chance to be good again? What will this require Amir to do?

Supplementary Activities

1. Use the Metaphors and Similes chart (see page 30 of this guide) to write at least one simile and one metaphor from this section. Include an interpretation for each example, and tell what things are being compared. This is an ongoing assignment for each section and will include both similes and metaphors when applicable. Examples: **Similes**—"...attention shifted to him like sunflowers turning to the sun" (p. 13); "I felt as if I were sitting on a pair of tree trunks" (p. 16); **Metaphors**—teachers (mullahs): self-righteous monkeys (p. 17); words: secret doorways (p. 30)

2. Working in a small group, locate and circle the city of Kabul on a map of Afghanistan. This is an ongoing assignment as different locations are identified throughout the book.

3. Write a paragraph in which you agree or disagree with Baba's belief that theft is the only sin.

Chapters Five–Seven

Afghanistan becomes a republic after a bloodless coup ends the monarchy. Amir is threatened by the local bully, Assef, but Hassan comes to his rescue, bravely brandishing his slingshot. A doctor fixes Hassan's cleft lip, and in the winter of 1975, Amir and Hassan enter the kite-fighting tournament. Amir becomes very worried that he will disappoint Baba, who shares his interest in kite-fighting. However, Amir displays great skill, and with Hassan's help he emerges triumphant. When Hassan recovers the last fallen kite for Amir as a trophy, he is confronted by Assef, who decides that Hassan can keep the kite for a "price." Assef brutally rapes Hassan, and Amir secretly witnesses the incident, choosing not to intervene.

Vocabulary

coup d'état
monarchy
republic
sociopath
hierarchy
nuances
integrity
viable
morose
sallow
beneficent
guileless

Discussion Questions

1. Discuss the closing statement in Chapter Four, "Because suddenly Afghanistan changed forever" (p. 34). How do Amir, Hassan, Ali, and Baba initially react to this change, and what is its significance? *(The sounds of gunfire, a siren, shattered glass, and people in the street signal the bloodless coup in which Daoud Khan ends the 40-year reign of King Zahir Shah in Afghanistan. Daoud replaces the monarchy with a republic form of government. Ali, Hassan, and Amir are together when the sounds begin, and Ali tries to reassure the frightened boys by telling them it is only duck hunters. Baba arrives after hours of delay, obviously fearful for the others' safety. Although life in Afghanistan changes very little initially, this night marks the "beginning of the end" [p. 36] of life as they have known it.)*

2. What does the simile "…he walked the neighborhood like a Khan strolling through his land…" (p. 38) indicate about Assef? Discuss Amir and Hassan's encounter with him in Chapter Five. What does this incident reveal about each boy? *(Assef thinks of himself as the ruler of the neighborhood and acts as if it belongs to him. Assef admires Hitler and wants Pashtuns to rid Afghanistan of Hazaras. Assef taunts and threatens Amir and Hassan because he does not think Pashtuns should associate with Hazaras, whom he regards as inferior. Assef displays sociopathic behavior. Hassan displays his unwavering loyalty and love for Amir by placing himself in harm's way to defend Amir. Amir, in stark contrast, nearly blurts out that Hassan is not his friend but his servant. This moment highlights Amir's flawed integrity and classist/racist tendencies.)*

3. Tell why winter is Amir's favorite season, and interpret the metaphor, "Kites were the one paper-thin slice of intersection between those spheres" (p. 49). *(Like many kids in Afghanistan, Amir does not have to go to school during the winter months. This means there is plenty of time for Hassan and Amir to play cards, watch movies, build snowmen, and fly kites. It is also the one time of year that Amir feels close to his father. For the rest of the year, Amir and Baba exist in different spheres, but kite flying provides a way for them to connect because it is something in which they both take a great interest and something at which they both excel.)*

4. Name several instances in this section in which Amir envies Hassan. In each case, is Amir's jealousy justified or not? *(Answers will vary but may include Ali hugging Hassan after they hear*

gunfire outside, Baba showing sympathy for Hassan's harelip, Baba buying the boys identical kites, and Hassan displaying natural athletic ability while in pursuit of a kite.)

5. Analyze the metaphor comparing Amir and Hassan's interaction to the game of "insect torture." What is the "other face" Amir sees when he asks Hassan if he would eat dirt for him? *(In response to Hassan's telling Amir he would rather eat dirt than lie to him, Amir finds pleasure in teasing Hassan, just as he does when he taunts him about a big word. He compares his actions toward Hassan to "insect torture," a game in which they would hold an insect under a magnifying glass. Amir often feels inferior to Hassan, but one way in which he levels the playing field is with meanness, something of which Hassan is incapable, both because of his natural disposition and class. Like the ant under the magnifying glass, Hassan is rendered helpless before Amir, as he feels it is his duty to agree to whatever Amir asks of him. Answers will vary, but it is reasonable to say that the "other face" that Amir sees is not that of his old friend Hassan but that of his servant.)*

6. What emotions does Amir experience before the kite tournament? What is Hassan's response? Refer to the simile, "I felt like a soldier trying to sleep in the trenches the night before a major battle" (p. 50). *(The night before the kite tournament, Amir feels like a soldier going to war because, to him, the kite tournament is war. Because Baba has won kite tournaments, Amir is determined to win the tournament in 1975 to prove to his father that he, too, is a winner. He yearns for Baba's approval and believes winning the kite tournament will cause Baba to treat him as a person instead of a ghost in their home. Amir thinks that winning the tournament may be enough to gain Baba's forgiveness for killing his mother. His fear of failure causes Amir to consider dropping out of the tournament, but Hassan reminds him of a dream he had in which they prove to everyone that a monster does not exist. Hassan calms Amir by telling him to remember that there is no monster.)*

7. Discuss the aftermath of the kite-fighting tournament, and assess Amir's initial reaction to Assef's attack on Hassan. Why does Amir decide not to help Hassan? *(Seeing Baba on the roof cheering for him is the single greatest moment of Amir's life. Amir sees Baba signaling for them to retrieve the last fallen kite, and Hassan runs off in pursuit of it. Amir has visions of presenting the blue kite to Baba as a trophy of his success. When Amir catches up with Hassan, Hassan is holding the kite and preparing to defend himself against Assef and his two allies. None of the boys see Amir. When Hassan refuses to give up the kite, Assef decides that the cost for keeping the kite will be Hassan's dignity. Amir is horrified as he watches Assef rape Hassan, and he realizes that he has one last chance to stand up for Hassan. Instead, he runs, partly because he is a coward but primarily because, in a world where "nothing [is] free," he is willing to sacrifice Hassan for the "key to Baba's heart" [p. 71], the last fallen kite. In the moment Amir rationalizes the rape in the same way that Assef does: Hassan is, after all, "just a Hazara." In other words, if Hazaras are inferior to Pashtuns, then their dignity is not worth as much as the dignity of Pashtuns. Both Hassan's and Amir's dignity are being threatened by Assef [Amir's in the form of the trophy kite], but Amir's line of thinking seems to be that, because of the difference in class/race, whatever humiliation Hassan may suffer at Assef's hands will not be as great and/or as important as what he may suffer if he returns home without the kite. This thought reveals that the classist/racist attitudes ingrained in Amir since he was very young are as much a part of his decision to not intervene as his jealousy of Hassan and his fear of Assef/losing the kite.)*

8. Explain the symbolism of the memories and the dream Amir recalls as Hassan is attacked. *(Amir remembers what Ali said about the brotherhood he and Hassan formed by feeding at the same breast. He also recalls visiting a fortuneteller who returned Hassan's money rather than reveal what he saw in Hassan's future. As the fortuneteller reads Amir's palm, a rooster crows [as in the Biblical story where Peter denies knowing Jesus to protect himself, Matthew 26: 69–75], and Amir withdraws his hand. In his dream, Amir is lost in a snowstorm and a hand [Hassan's, bloody from holding*

the kite string] reaches out and saves him. The memories reiterate the enormity of Amir's choice, betraying someone who has always been like a brother to him, and the dream symbolizes Hassan's loyalty, i.e., his willingness to "pay the price" to bring Amir the blue kite.)

9. Why does Amir compare Hassan to the lamb he saw sacrificed on Eid Al-Adha? *(Eid Al-Adha is a religious festival Muslims celebrate to commemorate Ibrahim's ["Abraham" in the Bible] willingness to sacrifice his son for God. As he watches Assef rape Hassan, he sees the same look in Hassan's eyes as he had seen in the lamb's as it was being sacrificed, a look of resignation. Hassan becomes the "sacrificial lamb" for Amir's desire to please his father.)*

10. Do you think Hassan knows that Amir witnessed the rape? Explain. What does Amir's behavior in the aftermath of the rape indicate about him? *(Answers will vary, but in the past Hassan has demonstrated that he is very perceptive and that he frequently knows what Amir is feeling, such as when Amir was pitying Hassan for imagining himself in the same hut his whole life. Whether students attribute Amir's failure to discuss the incident to immaturity or to selfish detachment, his concern for the kite's condition, ability to ignore the blood drops in the snow [foreshadowed by his dream], and the ease with which he forgets his betrayal once with Baba are worthy of discussion.)*

Supplementary Activities

1. Working with a partner, research and write a report about the causes, effects, and treatment of a cleft lip (harelip).

2. Write a poem of 12–16 lines in which you tell the story of Hassan as the "sacrificial lamb."

3. Add one simile and one metaphor to your list. Examples: **Similes**—"…hope grew in my heart, like snow collecting on a wall, one flake at a time" (p. 64); "His sightless eyes are like molten silver embedded in…craters" (p. 73); **Metaphors**—kite: gun (p. 50); Amir: ghost (p. 56)

Chapters Eight–Ten

Amir does not tell anyone what happened to Hassan. Hassan is consumed by shame and Amir is consumed by guilt, and their relationship rapidly deteriorates as a result. Amir's thirteenth birthday party is tainted by a visit from Assef and the knowledge that Baba would not have thrown such an extravagant party had it not been for Amir's triumph at the kite-fighting tournament. Overwhelmed by guilt, Amir decides that he must find a way to make Ali and Hassan leave Kabul. Amir falsely accuses Hassan of theft, and though Baba forgives Hassan immediately, Hassan and Ali decide to leave anyway. Baba is crushed. More than five years pass, and Baba and Amir make a harrowing journey from Afghanistan to Pakistan amidst political unrest.

Discussion Questions

1. Discuss Amir's trip to Jalalabad with his father, contrasting his expectations with the reality. Why does Amir feel as "empty as (the) unkempt pool" (p. 85)? *(When Amir asks his father to take him to Jalalabad, he envisions a wonderful trip for just the two of them, but Baba invites numerous relatives and Rahim Khan to go with them. Amir ends up sandwiched between obnoxious twins, and the conversation is extremely noisy. Shortly after Baba brags about Amir's victory in the kite tournament, Amir becomes carsick and throws up, much to Baba's embarrassment. When they arrive in Jalalabad, Amir has no time alone with Baba, who spends his time visiting with the relatives and bragging repeatedly about the tournament. Amir feels empty because the burden of guilt he carries overshadows everything on the trip.)*

Vocabulary
unkempt
insomniac
periphery
pregnant
alter ego
mortal
bile
lucrative
elopement
rueful
encapsulated

2. Discuss the symbolism of the scene in which Amir throws pomegranates at Hassan. Why does Amir want Hassan to hit him, and why do you think Hassan refuses? *(Prior to Amir's betrayal, he and Hassan had spent some of their best days beneath the pomegranate tree near the cemetery; the tree was symbolic of their friendship. The Koran says that pomegranates grow in the gardens of Paradise, and the Prophet Mohammed said that eating pomegranates protects one from envy and hatred. However, Amir has allowed these elements to spoil his and Hassan's friendship, and the pomegranates he throws are described as "overripe"; i.e., like the boys' friendship, their time has passed. In pelting Hassan with pomegranates, the fruits of friendship become weapons in Amir's hands. The scene may be viewed as representing the death of their friendship by Amir's hand. Amir wants to be punished to be absolved of his sin. Answers will vary. Hassan is a nonviolent person, and his loyalty to Amir [as a friend and otherwise] means that he will never hit Amir. Moreover, Hassan may know why Amir wants him to retaliate and does not want to make Amir's redemption quite so easy.)*

3. Assess what Assef's interactions with his parents, Amir, Baba, and Hassan at the party reveal about him. What is the significance of the gift he gives Amir? *(Assef looms over his parents, standing between them with his arms on their shoulders as if they are his children. Their nervous demeanor seems to indicate that they are intimidated by their son. At the same time, Assef is obviously fully capable of endearing himself to those he views as powerful. Baba repeatedly addresses Assef as "jan," something he rarely does when speaking to Amir. Amir is left feeling rejected and incredulous. Whether or not Assef thinks Amir knows what he did is debatable [though his inclusion of Hassan in his volleyball invitation is curious], but he certainly means to make Amir uncomfortable. Assef is clearly enjoying himself, especially as he teases Hassan, who must serve him and Wali drinks. Assef, as is characteristic of sociopaths, derives pleasure from manipulating others. His gift, a biography of Hitler, is significant as a symbol of everything he hopes to be—powerful, charismatic, merciless, and hateful. Amir continues to walk the line between good and evil, quietly rejecting the book but not standing up to Assef.)*

4. Examine the implications of Rahim Khan's conversation with Amir at his birthday party. Why is Rahim's gift important to Amir? *(Rahim tells Amir about his forbidden teenage love for a Hazara. Rahim reveals this to Amir to "open the door" for Amir to tell him about Hassan. Rahim does not want Amir to look back with regret, and he understands how difficult it can sometimes be to reconcile what one's conscience says with what society says. Rahim gives Amir a leather-bound notebook in which he can write his stories, indicating his love for Amir and his confidence in his future as a writer. This is the only gift that does not seem like "blood money" [Hassan's blood] to Amir; i.e., he thinks he would never have received the other gifts if he had not won the kite tournament.)*

5. What do Ali and Hassan give Amir for his birthday? How does Amir react to this gift? *(They give Amir a new, expensive copy of the* Shahnamah. *Ali tells Amir the book is not worthy of him, but Amir knows it is he who is unworthy. He tosses the book with the other gifts but, because the sight of it troubles him, he finally buries it at the bottom of the pile. This is the turning point for Amir's decision to accuse Hassan of lying and thus get rid of his "problem." It is symbolically the beginning of Amir's efforts to bury the past.)*

6. How does Baba react to Ali and Hassan's decision to leave? What do you think Baba thinks is their reason for leaving? Why do you think Amir is not moved enough to tell the truth or try to stop them from leaving? *(Baba pleads with them not to leave and cries. Answers will vary.)*

7. Describe the incident at the first checkpoint. What does it reveal about Baba and Amir? *(A young Russian soldier demands a half hour alone with a young woman as the price to let them pass. In spite of her tears and her husband's pleading, he refuses to back down. Baba intervenes and appeals to his sense of shame, but the soldier threatens to shoot him. Baba is willing to die in an attempt to protect the woman's honor. Unlike Amir, Baba shows himself to be a man of courage and strong convictions. Years after the shocking turn of events that destroyed his friendship with Hassan, Amir remains overly concerned with self-preservation. Unlike Amir, Baba knows that ignoring seemingly isolated incidents of evil allows it to spread like a cancer.)*

8. What is ironic about the fate that has befallen Kamal since the last time Amir saw him? What is ironic about Baba's attempt to console Kamal's father after Kamal dies? *(Kamal was one of the boys who helped hold down Hassan while Assef raped him. Since Amir last saw him, Kamal has himself been raped and appears to be permanently traumatized. If Baba knew that Kamal was instrumental in tearing apart his own family years ago, Baba would not be attempting to comfort Kamal's father, who has just lost the last of his immediate family.)*

9. **Prediction:** What will happen to Baba and Amir now?

Supplementary Activities

1. Working with a small group, trace the route of escape into Pakistan by locating the following places on a map of Afghanistan and Pakistan: Kabul, Jalalabad, Khyber Pass, and Peshawar.

2. Working in a small group, reenact one of the following scenes: Baba and Amir's conversation with Assef, the conversation between Amir and Rahim Khan at the party, Baba's confrontation with Ali and Hassan about the alleged theft, and the confrontation at the first checkpoint.

3. Continue adding to your simile/metaphor list. Examples: **Similes**—"turrets swiveling like accusing fingers" (p. 113); "The husband's face had become as pale as the moon…" (p. 115); **Metaphors**—Amir: snake in the grass, monster in the lake (p. 105); memory: morsel of a good past, brushstroke of color (p. 123)

Chapters Eleven–Thirteen

Baba and Amir go to America, and Baba works at a gas station. Amir graduates from high school, and Baba buys Amir a car. Amir attends college, and he and Baba earn extra money by selling used goods at a flea market, where Amir meets and falls in love with Soraya. Baba develops terminal lung cancer and acknowledges Amir's writing talent. Baba dies shortly after Amir and Soraya marry. Soraya and Amir struggle with their inability to have a child. Amir has two books published.

Discussion Questions

1. Compare/contrast Baba's expectation of America with the reality he faces when he arrives in California. Correlate his and Amir's individual reactions to life in America with the following literary devices: "Baba was like the widower who remarries but can't let go of his dead wife" (p. 129); "…Kabul had become a city of ghosts for me. A city of harelipped ghosts" (p. 136); "America was a river…" (p. 136). *(Baba loved the idea of achieving the "American dream," but actually living in America proves very stressful and frustrating for him. In Afghanistan, his word was his bond; in America, he must provide identification to pay with a check. He and Amir must*

Vocabulary
de facto
cretin
acrid
coyly
tenets
chastity
kiosk
pulmonary
pathology
palliative
oncologist
mosque
chagrin
overt
ambivalent

adjust from a lavish lifestyle in Afghanistan to struggling to survive on Baba's salary from a menial job. Afghanistan is Baba's first and only love, and for him America [his "second wife"] pales in comparison. In contrast, Amir has no desire to return to Kabul and is glad to be far from reminders of Hassan [the "ghosts"]. Amir embraces life in America, immerses himself in it, and, at least temporarily, is able to drown his sins.)

2. Discuss Baba's celebration for Amir's high school graduation, and analyze what this reveals about him and Amir. Examine the universality of the conflict between Baba and Amir over Amir's plans for the future. *(Baba states that he is proud of Amir, and this fulfills the yearning Amir has always had for his father's approval. Baba takes him to an Afghan kabob house and later to a bar where he brags about Amir and becomes the center of attention, much as he often was in Afghanistan. Baba's gift of an old car elicits tears of deep appreciation from Amir, in contrast to his blasé reaction to the elaborate bicycle he received on his thirteenth birthday. Baba and Amir now live far more leanly than they did in Afghanistan, and this is a gift that could not have been easy for Baba to give. It is a night of triumph for both father and son: Baba gives as much as he can to Amir; at the same time there is the implicit acknowledgment that it does not matter that Baba can no longer provide as much for his son as he used to because Amir has come into his own and can take care of himself. Like many young people, Amir wants to follow his dream [become a writer], and like many parents, Baba wants his child to do something which promises to be lucrative and secure, like becoming a doctor or a lawyer, professions which Baba considers "real work.")*

3. Discuss Baba's business venture at the flea market, and assess its importance to him and Amir. *(In order to improve their finances, Baba buys an old Volkswagen bus, and they begin a weekly trip to garage sales. They buy a variety of items that they take to the flea market on Sunday and resell at a profit. Afghan families work an entire section of the flea market, and Baba finds the camaraderie he has been missing in America. Baba introduces Amir to General Taheri, whom he had known in Afghanistan. Amir meets and is intrigued by Taheri's daughter, Soraya, whom he thinks of as his Swap Meet Princess.)*

4. How does Amir and Soraya's relationship develop? Note the differences in American and Afghan courtship practices. *(Amir makes it a point to drop by the Taheri booth when the general is away, and he and Soraya develop a friendship. This is against Afghan tradition, and Baba cautions Amir to be careful because Taheri, a Pashtun, will protect his daughter's chastity at all costs. Soraya's mother is friendly to Amir, but her father is against any type of ongoing relationship between his daughter and Amir. When Amir brings Soraya one of the short stories he has written, her father throws it in the trash and cautions Amir about doing anything that will cause gossip.)*

5. How does Baba behave in the aftermath of his cancer diagnosis? Why do you think he behaves this way? How does the diagnosis affect Amir? *(Baba's behavior is mercurial, and he refuses any treatment that will prolong his life. He continues his routines [like working at the gas station and the flea market] for as long as he possibly can and forbids Amir to tell anyone that he is ill. Baba is a proud man and likes to be in control. For the first time he feels utterly vulnerable, and he does not know how to handle it. He knows his death will be a slow process anyway, and he does not see the point in prolonging it any further. He chooses the path that seems to afford him the most dignity and the least amount of suffering. Amir is stunned to find himself in the role of caretaker and realizes that he will be completely on his own soon, and this scares him.)*

6. Name some ways that Baba shows his love for Amir before he dies. How is Baba remembered by those who attend his funeral? Do you think that Amir can live up to Baba's legacy? *(Despite his frail condition, Baba goes to the Taheris' home to ask the general for his blessing in the matter of Soraya and Amir's marriage. He attends the engagement party and spends most of his life savings [$35,000] on the wedding. In his final days he even takes an interest in Amir's stories, something for which Amir has waited his whole life. Baba is remembered as an unselfish and generous man, a giver. Everyone has something to say about how he helped them at one time or another. Answers will vary.)*

7. Why do you think the general forbids Jamila to sing? Why do you think Jamila is so fond of Amir? *(Answers will vary. The general's official position is that singing is beneath Jamila. However, the general obviously does not think music is beneath him—he owns a considerable music collection. It would seem that the proud general simply does not want to be upstaged by his wife. Indeed Soraya indicates that Afghan women are held to harsher standards than men and that these standards may contradict the standards to which men are held. The general seems emotionally detached from Jamila, and she is probably very glad to have someone like Amir who listens to her and takes her concerns seriously.)*

8. In what ways do you think Soraya and Amir are similar? How are they different? Why doesn't Amir care about her past? *(Like Amir, Soraya has a proud father who likes to be in control, and she sometimes has trouble getting along with him. The general feels that her talents could have been put to better use in a more lucrative profession, and Soraya has a past of which she is not proud. However, Soraya is more courageous and honest than Amir, and she has taken steps to put her past behind her. Amir doesn't care about her past because he knows all about regret, especially since his secret is bigger and unresolved.)*

9. Do you think that Amir deserves to be happy? Do you think that he and Soraya are unable to have a child because Amir is being punished for his sins? *(Answers will vary.)*

10. **Prediction:** Will Amir and Soraya eventually have a child? If not, will they decide to adopt?

Supplementary Activities

1. Working in a small group, reenact Amir and Soraya's wedding.

2. Working with a partner, research current information about lung cancer. Present an oral report to the class about its causes, treatment, and prognosis.

3. Continue adding to your simile/metaphor list. Examples: **Similes**—"shoulder blade felt like a bird's wing" (p. 161); "the sofa, set on the stage like a throne" (p. 171); **Metaphors**—bus: sad carcass of rusted metal (p. 137); Soraya: Swap Meet Princess (p. 144)

Chapters Fourteen–Nineteen

Amir receives the phone call from Rahim Khan, asking him to come to Pakistan. Their conversation makes Amir realize that Rahim knows he betrayed Hassan. Amir goes to Pakistan where Rahim, who is deathly ill, tells him about Hassan and gives him a letter that Hassan wrote to Amir. Rahim reveals that Ali was killed years ago by a land mine and that Hassan was killed recently by the Taliban. He also tells Amir that Hassan was actually his half-brother. Rahim asks Amir to go to Afghanistan and rescue Hassan's son, Sohrab, from an orphanage and bring him to a family in Pakistan. Amir reluctantly agrees to go and meets Rahim's friend, Farid, who will be his driver while he is in Afghanistan. Amir is shocked by the current state of his country and is welcomed into the home of Farid's brother, Wahid.

Vocabulary

- soliloquies
- garrulous
- collateral damage
- melancholic
- pragmatic
- affable
- empathy
- snickered
- jihad
- cursory
- impregnated

Discussion Questions

1. Discuss Rahim Khan's phone call to Amir, and evaluate its effect on him. Note the significance of Rahim's statement, "There is a way to be good again" (p. 192). *(Rahim, who is very sick, asks Amir to come to Pakistan. His allusion to a way to be good again makes Amir realize that Rahim has always known that he betrayed Hassan. The night after the phone call, Amir dreams of Hassan running in the snow yelling "For you, a thousand times over!" This sets the stage for what Amir will learn in Pakistan and the decision he will make in order to redeem himself.)*

2. Why do you think Hosseini decided that Rahim Khan should narrate Chapter Sixteen? *(Though Amir could have summarized what Rahim told him, hearing Rahim's distinct voice and his emotional impressions of events in Afghanistan during the preceding 20 years gives the reader a palpable sense of time, and life, lost. Much of the story has been devoted to ensconcing the reader in the very different life Amir has built for himself in America, all but erasing his childhood. Rahim is Amir's last living connection to his old life and family, and his testimony reminds Amir [and the reader] of why it once was and still is important.)*

3. Discuss Rahim's rationale for staying in Kabul under both the Northern Alliance and the Taliban rule. *(Kabul is his home and, even though life under the Northern Alliance was hazardous and oppressive, he stayed in his own area of Kabul and tried to avoid danger. The people of Kabul considered the Taliban to be heroes and danced in the streets when they kicked the Alliance out, greeting the Taliban and having their pictures taken with them. Only later would they realize the terrible price the Taliban would exact for "peace.")*

4. Examine the contents of Hassan's letter to Amir, noting what it reveals about Hassan. How does the letter affect Amir? *(Hassan begins his letter by telling Amir he has told his wife and son about their friendship. He reveals the devastation and fear of living in Kabul under the Taliban rule. He tells Amir about Sohrab and reminds Amir of how he loved to hear Amir read the* Shahnamah. *He mentions Rahim's grave illness and his fear that Rahim will not live very long. He concludes by mentioning nightmares he has been having. Significantly, he has been dreaming about hanged corpses rotting in soccer fields and blood-red grass, a scene similar to what Amir will see in the Ghazi Stadium. He concludes by saying that he also has good dreams about his son and about Amir returning to Kabul. Hassan refers to himself as Amir's "faithful friend." Hassan clearly has an extraordinary capacity for forgiveness. Amir realizes that Hassan is still the same loyal friend he was as a child and that he does not hate him for his sin of betrayal.)*

5. How does Amir react to the news of Hassan's death? How is Hassan's death ironic? *(When Amir learns that both Hassan and Farzana died because Hassan tried to protect the estate in Kabul, Amir, overcome with grief, can only whisper "no" repeatedly. Amir thinks of everyone who was in Hassan's hospital room years ago and realizes that he will soon be the only one left. Hassan's entire life was one of loyalty and devotion, and he showed complete, unquestioning respect for the class divisions. He died defending his master's estate, but the Taliban killed him and his wife under the pretense that they were living in the home [something Hassan had steadfastly refused to do].)*

6. How does Rahim convince Amir to help Sohrab? What is Amir's response, and what do you think it indicates about him? Do you think Amir would have decided to help Sohrab if Rahim had not told him that Hassan was his half-brother? *(Rahim tries to remind Amir that life in Afghanistan did not stop after he left. His account of the last 20 years paints a moving portrait of his, Hassan's, and Afghanistan's ups and downs. Rahim lets Amir know that he believes in him and that Hassan continued to believe in him as well. He tells Amir that Hassan's loyalty to the family got him killed. Amir has lived for 26 years with the guilt of betraying Hassan, yet even after hearing that it is Rahim's dying wish that he help Sohrab, Amir does not want to look for the boy. Answers will vary, but Amir certainly appears ungrateful and self-centered. Some students may say that had Amir had more time to think after Rahim's account, he would have done the right thing eventually. However, as written, Amir says that he cannot rescue Sohrab because he would risk losing the life he has built in America. Amir does not consider that his actions may have cost Hassan his chance at the kind of life he enjoys until it is revealed that they are half-brothers. It seems that Amir is inclined to do the right thing, but only after every other option has been exhausted.)*

7. Baba's guiding principle in life was to never steal from anyone. He was quoted as saying, "There is only one sin. And that is theft…When you tell a lie, you steal someone's right to the truth" (p. 225). In light of what Amir learns about Hassan, do you think Baba was a hypocrite? *(Answers will vary. Baba made the biggest mistake of his life when he slept with Sanaubar. Like Amir, Baba betrayed someone who would have given his life for him and stole his honor. However, as Rahim suggests, Baba may only have kept the truth from Hassan and Amir in order to protect them. Afghan society, as depicted here, would not have tolerated such an indiscretion. One could argue that Baba chose not to tell the boys simply because it would ruin his reputation, of which he was quite proud. However, it seems unlikely that it was only for vanity that Baba kept his indiscretion secret. Baba spent his life doing good and charitable works, and many of the things he did may have been very difficult or impossible to accomplish had he been shamed for his indiscretion.)*

8. Explain why Farid does not like Amir at first. *(Farid barely suppresses his hostility toward Amir at the beginning of their trip and scoffs at Amir's reference to Afghanistan as his country. Farid had joined the jihad against the Soviets and had lost his father and two children as well as some of his toes and fingers. Farid sees himself as someone who has been loyal to his country through its trials and tribulations and looks with disdain on the "easy" life he feels Amir has been living in America. He believes Amir only wants to get to Kabul to sell his father's land and take his money back to America.)*

9. While at Wahid's home, what evidence is there that Amir truly is an "honorable man" and a "true Afghan"? *(Wahid wants to know what brings Amir back to Afghanistan, and Amir explains to him that he is there to find the son of his "illegitimate half-brother," who meant a lot to him. In telling Wahid this, he makes no secret of the fact that Hassan and Sohrab are Hazaras. This is the first time that Amir has spoken honestly with someone outside of his family about who Hassan is and what he means to him. It is an important moment in the novel because Amir seems finally to embrace both Hassan's and his own identity without prejudice. Later, when Amir thinks that the*

children are looking at his watch, he gives it to them. When he realizes that they were actually staring at his food, he places a fistful of money under a mattress, much as he had done 26 years before in Ali's hut. As in the incident 26 years earlier, the motive seems to be guilt, yet this time Amir's actions are honorable rather than disgraceful.)

10. Compare Amir's dream near the end of the section with his earlier mental picture of Hassan's death, and analyze the symbolism of this dream. *(Just as in his earlier mental picture, Amir sees Hassan kneeling on the street. In the dream, however, Hassan is muttering "For you a thousand times over" under his breath. The man in the herringbone vest and black turban fires the rifle at Hassan's head. Amir realizes that he is the executioner. Symbolically, Amir "killed" Hassan in 1975 when he failed to defend him against Assef. The dream is significant because it is a sign that Amir is finally ready to take responsibility for his actions 26 years ago.)*

11. **Prediction:** Will Amir be able to find and rescue Sohrab?

Supplementary Activities

1. Working with a partner, reenact the dialogue between Rahim Khan and Amir in which Rahim reveals the truth about Hassan's birth.

2. Sketch your interpretation of one or both of the similes with which Amir describes Afghanistan: "little villages sprouting…like discarded toys among the rocks…men sitting on their haunches, like a row of crows" (p. 231).

3. Continue adding to your simile/metaphor list. Examples: **Similes**—"his life of…loyalty drifting from him like the…kites he used to chase" (p. 219); "I felt like a man sliding down a steep cliff…" (p. 222); **Metaphor**—sleep, book: savior (p. 193)

Chapters Twenty–Twenty-Two

Amir and Farid arrive in Kabul, and Amir is shocked by the changes in the city. Amir sees his first "Beard Patrol," and Farid cautions him about his actions around the Talibs. The two men locate the orphanage and discover that a Talib official has taken Sohrab. Amir visits his childhood home, and he and Farid attend a soccer game at the Ghazi Stadium, where they see public executions carried out by the Talib who has Sohrab. They arrange a meeting with the Talib, who turns out to be Assef. Sohrab has been subject to Assef's abuse, and Amir fights Assef for the right to take the boy. Amir is nearly killed, but he and Sohrab manage to escape to Farid's truck after Sohrab makes good on his father's threat to take out Assef's eye.

Discussion Questions

1. For Amir, how is "returning to Kabul…like running into an old, forgotten friend and seeing that life hadn't been good to him…" (p. 246)? *(Amir is as appalled at the changes in Kabul as he would be meeting a friend after many years and seeing him homeless and destitute. He does not recognize the city of his childhood. Everywhere he looks, he sees rubble and beggars who are mostly small children. The dearth of adult males signifies the innumerable men who have died in wars under the different regimes. Collapsed buildings and debris litter the streets, and the trees have been cut down for firewood.)*

2. Discuss what Amir learns about his mother and how this affects him. *(The old beggar, Dr. Rasul, had once been a professor at the university where Amir's mother taught and had known her well. He comments on her beauty and dignity, things she enjoyed, and how she felt about her pregnancy. Dr. Rasul mentions that she feared that because she was so profoundly happy, something would be taken away from her. Baba never described Sofia in detail, and this new information makes Amir feel closer to his mother.)*

Vocabulary

unadulterated
gingerly
mosaic
cleric
sanctity
Mecca
guru
furtive
surreal
epiphany
bourgeoisie

3. How is Amir received at the orphanage? How can Zaman afford to keep the orphanage running? How does Zaman justify his actions, and do you think there is any other way to handle such a difficult situation? *(Zaman is at first suspicious of Amir and denies knowing Sohrab. However, Amir convinces Zaman that his intentions are honorable by revealing details about Sohrab and telling him that he is his half-uncle. Zaman periodically sells a child to a Talib who uses the children for his sexual perversion. Zaman feels justified in allowing the Talib to buy children because this gives him money to feed and provide a home for many other children. Answers will vary, but Zaman does seem to have sacrificed a lot to keep the orphanage running, and the way in which he receives Amir seems to indicate that he does care about the children.)*

4. What evidence is there of the Taliban's cruelty in Kabul? *(Answers will vary. Farid cautions Amir to keep his eyes on his feet when the Talibs are near, and the old beggar tells Amir they are just looking for someone to kill. Amir sees the dead body of a young man who had been publicly executed still hanging from the beam of a restaurant. Farid points out two men haggling over the price of an artificial leg one of them is trying to sell to the other. When a scrawny boy tries to sell him some "sexy pictures" [which are actually not risqué by most standards], Farid tells him that, if he is caught, the Taliban will flog him mercilessly. At the soccer game in Ghazi Stadium, young whip-toting Talibs roam the aisles and strike anyone who cheers too loudly, and two people are publicly executed.)*

5. Examine what Amir finds when he returns to his childhood home. Analyze the symbolism of the house, the pomegranate tree, and the carving. How is this scene significant? *(The house is in disrepair, symbolic of Afghanistan's fallen splendor and Amir's lost childhood. Everywhere Amir looks, something reminds him of Hassan. He goes to the hilltop and finds the pomegranate tree, now wilted and barren, a symbol of his wasted friendship with Hassan. He finds the carving, "Amir and Hassan, the Sultans of Kabul" [p. 27], faded but still visible in the trunk of the tree. The carving symbolizes Amir and Hassan's friendship, which is barely perceptible but still exists. Amir has tried to forget for the past 26 years, but he now wants to remember. The scene is significant because it may be the first time that Amir truly appreciates the friendship/childhood he gave up.)*

6. Explain the irony of the simile referring to the Talib, "…his arms spread like those of Jesus on the cross" (p. 271). *(The simile is ironic since Jesus sacrificed himself for others, and this man sacrifices others for himself.)*

7. Why do you think Hosseini decided that Assef should grow up to be a high-ranking Talib? *(This decision represents the culmination of a larger point Hosseini makes about the Taliban. Assef is not a pious man; he is a sociopath who uses a guise of piety to manipulate others to his satisfaction. As a youth he hated Hazaras, not for any religious reasons, but because of deep-seated, racist/classist attitudes. He admired Hitler and later became an integral part of the Hazara massacres. As a youth he was a bully who took pleasure in making others suffer, and he has grown into a monster who cares only about pleasing himself, usually at the expense of others. Assef's defining characteristic is his debauched and savage nature, his lack of empathy. This lack of empathy is what separates sociopaths from other human beings, and it is the challenge of the sociopath to hide this glaring flaw*

so that he/she may seem to others to be benign, caring, or even just [as in Assef's case] so that he/she can continue to prey on others. Hosseini implies that this—not a truly dedicated Muslim—is the type of person who aligns himself with the Taliban. Assef says of his position, "I'm in my element" [p. 281]. By making Assef a high-ranking Talib, Hosseini robs the Taliban of credibility and casts them as hateful brutes.)

8. Analyze the metaphor, "They (Sohrab's eyes) were slaughter sheep's eyes" (p. 285). How does this description relate to the description of Hassan on page 76? *(When Amir tells Assef he wants the boy, Sohrab's eyes flick to Amir and he sees in them the same resignation he saw in a sacrificial lamb's just before its throat was cut. This is the same look he saw in Hassan's eyes as Assef raped him. The fact that Sohrab has the same look in his eyes would seem to imply that he, too, has been a victim of Assef's abuse, a martyr for the unjust class system, Assef's perverted desires and wrongful sense of entitlement, and Amir's sins from long ago. Sohrab's eyes seem to plead with Amir, and Amir knows that he must pay the cost to save this lamb from any further sacrifice.)*

9. Discuss Amir's fight with Assef. Why does Amir laugh? How is the way in which Amir is saved ironic? *(Using his brass knuckles, Assef brutally beats Amir, who has never fought anyone in his life. Amir is violently thrown around the room as his bones and teeth are broken, but he laughs because, for the first time since the winter of 1975, he feels at peace. In risking his life for Sohrab, Amir finally defends Hassan as he should have in 1975 and takes responsibility for his actions 26 years ago. The punishment he receives at Assef's hands is his penance for those sins, and he is relieved of the guilt he has carried for so long. As with Assef, some suffering is necessary for Amir's "stone" to pass. Sohrab saves Amir with his slingshot—just as Hassan once did—and Sohrab follows through on the threat his father made so many years ago by knocking out Assef's eye.)*

10. **Prediction:** Will Amir and Sohrab successfully escape?

Supplementary Activities

1. Working in a small group, use your map to trace Amir's route back into Afghanistan. Mark his stops along the way using markers or thumbtacks.
2. Write a metaphorical poem that describes Sohrab's reaction to Amir's beating.
3. Continue adding to your simile/metaphor list. Examples: **Similes**—"…his head swung side to side like a pendulum" (p. 280); "ribs snapping like…tree branches (p. 288); **Metaphors**—Jadeh Maywand: giant sand castle (p. 246); bodies of Hazaras: dog meat for dogs (p. 277)

Chapters Twenty-Three–Twenty-Four

Amir is treated for his serious injuries in the hospital in Peshawar while Farid looks after Sohrab. Amir receives a letter from Rahim Khan in which he confirms that he has always known of Amir's betrayal and tries to explain why Amir and Hassan were raised as they were. Farid reveals to Amir that Thomas and Betty Caldwell do not exist, and Amir and Sohrab go to Islamabad. Amir tells Sohrab that he is his half-uncle, and Sohrab slowly begins to trust Amir. Sohrab agrees to go live with Amir and Soraya, and Amir tells Soraya all about his past. Amir is unable to get official clearance to take Sohrab to the United States, and Sohrab attempts suicide when he thinks Amir will leave him in an orphanage in Pakistan. Soraya calls to say that her uncle Sharif will almost certainly be able to get Sohrab a humanitarian visa.

Vocabulary
pneumothorax
impunity
squalid
harried
milieu
asylum
nimbus
humanitarian visa

Discussion Questions

1. What are some ways that Hosseini communicates to the reader Amir's semi-conscious state at the beginning of Chapter Twenty-Three? *(Answers will vary, but some examples include Amir's inability to discern time passed or identify most people around him, the fact that the surgeons' faces "slip in and out of view" [p. 293], the lack of any dialogue between him and others, the repeated use of "I fade out," and the general use of inexact and stream-of-consciousness descriptions.)*

2. Discuss the significance of Amir's injuries. In what ways are the effects of Assef's assault on Amir similar to the effects of Assef's assault on Hassan? In what ways are they different? *(Amir almost dies. Amir is literally broken down and must be rebuilt, which is symbolic of the death of Amir's old self and his rebirth as a more empathetic, less self-centered person. The "harelip" Amir receives further emphasizes his connection to Hassan and the fact that the beating was his penance for betraying Hassan, someone he had once regarded as inferior due to class/race. Amir's experience is, in every way, a painful reminder that neither boy was more or less deserving of basic human dignity. Both assaults bring the victims close to death. Amir has a brush with physical death, while Hassan had a brush with spiritual death. Amir's assault frees him from many of his inner demons; Hassan's assault was to blame for most of his inner demons. Hassan stopped smiling not long after his harelip was fixed. Amir's smile may reflect profound happiness for the first time in many years after his harelip is fixed; Hassan had no loyal friends to help him recover from his assault; Sohrab and Farid's support is integral to Amir's recovery.)*

3. In Chapter Twenty-One, Farid asks, "You come all the way from America for…a Shi'a" (p. 267)? Do you think Farid meant for this question to have racist/classist undertones? *(Answers will vary. Some students may react as Amir did and assume that Farid is racist/classist. However, Farid may ask this question, at least in part, because he feels it is unusual for a Pashtun to care so deeply for a Hazara. It is worth noting that Farid is outraged by Zaman's admission that Sohrab is one of the children who was sold. Perhaps most significantly, without his loyalty and help, it seems unlikely that Amir could have successfully rescued Sohrab.)*

4. Using information revealed in Rahim Khan's letter, explain how Baba is partially responsible for the kind of boy/man that Amir became. *(Baba's internal conflict over his own flawed character meant that he was harder on Amir, in whom he saw himself. His inability to openly express fatherly love for Hassan resulted in a critical and resentful attitude toward his legitimate and "privileged" son, Amir. Consequently, Amir often felt rejected, particularly when he compared his father's treatment of him to his father's treatment of Hassan. Amir always longed to please his father but learned to expect rejection. He sometimes felt like an outcast in his own home, and this resulted in his becoming a distrustful and self-hating [but self-centered] person. Amir thought little of himself but thought even less of others. When the opportunity presented itself for Amir to win Baba's love, Amir found that he was willing to sacrifice Hassan to do so.)*

5. How is Amir able to forge a friendship with Sohrab? *(Their troubles with Assef lay the foundation for their friendship. Then as Amir recovers, he plays panjpar with Sohrab and tells Sohrab that he had played this game with Hassan. As they play, Amir relates other information about Hassan, and Sohrab responds with what Hassan had told him about Amir, e.g., that Amir was Hassan's best friend. Amir tells Sohrab he would like to be his friend. Later when Sohrab wanders off unexpectedly, Amir remembers how Sohrab was intrigued by the mosque and, with the hotel*

manager's help, Amir finds him there. Sohrab tells Amir about a trip he made with Hassan to the Blue Mosque in Mazar-i-Sharif, and they begin to talk about their parents. When Sohrab is worried that he is starting to forget his parents' faces, Amir gives him his picture of Hassan and Sohrab.)

6. Of what things is Sohrab ashamed? Why might Amir and Sohrab need each other? Do you think Rahim was justified in lying to Amir about Thomas and Betty Caldwell? *(Sohrab feels ashamed because of what Assef and his men did to him and because he hurt Assef, something of which he is at first unsure his father would have approved. Sohrab needs a father figure, someone who is proud of him and can reassure him. Amir needs someone who needs him so that he can do something selfless, "be good again," and take pride in himself. Answers will vary, but even with the lie, Rahim had a hard time convincing Amir to help Sohrab.)*

7. Why does Amir compare himself to Jean Valjean from *Les Miserables*? Why does Sohrab try to commit suicide? Do you think Amir should feel responsible for Sohrab's actions? *(Amir feels powerless in his struggle to give Sohrab a new life in the United States. Like Jean Valjean, a desperate man who is sentenced to prison for five years for stealing a loaf of bread, Amir is the victim of an unfair system. At first it appears that Amir will need to relinquish Sohrab to an orphanage in Pakistan, file an orphan petition, and go through the required home study. When Amir explains to Sohrab that he must stay in an orphanage for a while, Sohrab begs him not to put him there and reminds Amir of his promise. In spite of Amir's reassurance, Sohrab's fear of living in an orphanage [combined with the existing trauma with which he has been coping] is too much for him to bear, and he tries to kill himself. Answers will vary, but it is reasonable to say that Amir makes the best decisions he can with the options available to him. In making a promise he does not know if he can keep, Amir is, at worst, guilty of a moment of poor judgment. Unfortunately, the recent tragedies in Sohrab's life have left Sohrab too vulnerable to handle this difficult situation.)*

8. **Prediction:** Will Sohrab live, and will Amir find a way to bring him to America?

Supplementary Activities

1. Working in a small group, research one of the following: (a) the current INS directives for gaining permission to bring a child to America from a foreign country (b) the destruction of the giant Buddhas in Bamiyan (c) the cause/effect of Post-Traumatic Stress Syndrome. Give an oral report to the class. If your report is for (c), explain how the condition relates to Sohrab.

2. Working with a partner, reenact the mosque scene.

3. Continue adding to your simile/metaphor list. Examples: **Similes**—"mosque sparkled like a diamond" (p. 317); "…the air-conditioning hit my face like a splash of ice water" (p. 327); **Metaphor**—cabbies: sharks (p. 335)

Chapter Twenty-Five

Sohrab nearly dies in the hospital, and Amir prays for the first time in 15 years. Sohrab eventually recovers physically from his suicide attempt but remains emotionally withdrawn. Amir takes him to the United States, but he does not respond to Amir's and Soraya's love. When General Taheri asks whom he should tell the neighbors Sohrab is, Amir proudly acknowledges Sohrab as his nephew. Amir and Soraya raise money for a hospital on the Afghan-Pakistani border that helps land mine victims. Amir tells Sohrab about Hassan's kite-fighting and kite-running talents, and he and Sohrab fly a kite together. Sohrab smiles slightly for the first time in almost a year, and Amir runs a kite for him.

Vocabulary
benevolent
serpentine
protocol
myriad
catharsis
eccentric
melee

Discussion Questions

1. Amir suffers greatly while Sohrab is in critical condition in the hospital. In what ways is Amir's suffering significant? What motivates Amir's prayer, and what does his prayer indicate about how his character has changed? *(Amir's suffering is significant because it causes him to pray for the first time in 15 years. Perhaps more significant than the fact Amir prays is the manner in which he prays. Amir gets down on his knees on a makeshift prayer rug in front of everyone in the waiting room, not caring what others think of him. In this moment all that matters is Sohrab. It is true that Amir's prayer is partially motivated by guilt [since he desperately does not want Sohrab's blood on his hands], but Amir is genuinely worried about Sohrab's well-being. There is no one around to pressure Amir to do the right thing, yet Amir thinks nothing of sacrificing his pride in the interest of saving another human being. Furthermore, Amir promises God that he will pray all the time from now on, not just when he has a special request. Loss and the threat of loss have changed Amir. He has learned selflessness, gratitude, and humility.)*

2. How and why does Amir become "the one under the microscope" (p. 355)? *(Just as Amir once put Hassan's loyalty to the test, closely examining and scrutinizing him by asking Hassan if he would eat dirt for him, Sohrab now tests Amir's loyalty with his unresponsiveness. Sohrab probably felt that he had plenty of reasons to distrust Amir based on his recent experiences with people, but he eventually decided to trust Amir anyway. However, shortly after this, his trust in Amir was shaken when it seemed that Amir was going to break his promise. Sohrab becomes more distant than ever, allowing Amir to suffer for as long as is necessary to earn back his trust.)*

3. Why does it not bother Amir to think that Baba may have considered Hassan his "true son"? *(Amir has forgiven his father, so he is no longer a prisoner of anger. In addition, he has also forgiven himself, which means that he is no longer a prisoner of guilt and is able to love himself. He believes he is good and worthy of love, and in the end that is what is most important.)*

4. How does Amir respond to General Taheri's inquiry about Sohrab? What is significant about Amir's statement? *(Amir states flatly that Sohrab is his nephew as well as how this came to be. He tells the general that he is never to refer to Sohrab as "Hazara boy" in his presence. Amir shows courage and conviction as he stands up for Sohrab. By taking such a firm stance, Amir risks alienating the general and possibly the Afghan community. Amir again sacrifices himself in order to do what is right, and by proudly recognizing Sohrab as a full-fledged member of the family, he shows that he is no longer influenced by the racist and classist attitudes which have proven toxic in his country and his life. Amir's attitude toward life is one of love.)*

5. How does Amir cope with Sohrab's long silence? Why might this cause be close to Amir's heart, and what similarities between Amir and Baba does this new activity reveal? *(Amir immerses himself in a project that funds a hospital on the border of Afghanistan and Pakistan that helps land mine victims. Rahim Khan once commented that there is not a "more Afghan way of dying" [p. 206] than being killed by a land mine, so this is a way for Amir to give back and stay connected to his home country while continuing to live in America. His return to Afghanistan impressed upon him that his country needs him and that there is more to being a "true Afghan" than simply having grown up in Afghanistan. Also, Ali was killed by a land mine, and Amir once wondered if Hassan's and Ali's lives might have turned out completely different if they had not remained in Afghanistan. It is too late to help Ali, but Amir may feel moved to pursue this cause in honor of him. Amir seems to have grown into a man who is very similar to his father in that he has a son he does not quite know how to connect with, and to fill the void he feels, he gives back to his community.)*

6. What "small, wondrous thing" gives Amir hope? *(Amir tells Sohrab about Hassan's kite-fighting and kite-running talents, and as they fly a kite together, Sohrab's eyes become alert and lose their glassy, vacant look. Amir looks down at Sohrab and sees a tiny lopsided grin and an almost imperceptible nod when Amir asks if Sohrab wants him to run a kite for him.)*

7. How does Amir show his loyalty to Sohrab in the novel's final scene? What do Amir's actions reveal about him? *(In all the years Amir and Hassan worked together in kite fighting, Amir was always the one who flew the kite and Hassan was his assistant. Hassan ran the kite for him but always returned it to Amir, who got the "glory" for the win. Now Amir elevates Sohrab to his former role and demotes himself to Hassan's role. Answers will vary, but this humble and selfless act of loyalty to Sohrab [and symbolically, Hassan] is particularly notable because Amir is under no moral pressure to offer it.)*

Supplementary Activities

1. Write a five senses poem about Amir's long path to redemption.
2. Add to your simile/metaphor list. Examples: **Similes**—"…each breath is like inhaling fire (p. 345); "His skin is dark like…imported Swiss chocolate…" (p. 348); **Metaphors**—legs: blocks of concrete; heart: jackhammer (p. 345)

Post-reading Discussion Questions

1. One of the novel's major themes is the search for redemption. Carson McCullers once said that "…humiliation…is the square root of sin….The sin of hurting people's feelings…[is] the same as murder." Do you agree with this statement, and do you feel that Amir succeeded in redeeming himself? *(Answers will vary, but the idea of degrees of humiliation as well as intent [which the philosopher Immanuel Kant argued was the key to assessing the moral value of an action] should be part of the discussion. It is reasonable to say that while rape may be considered emotional murder [since the act's intrusive nature may irreparably damage the individual's sense of self], it was not Amir's intention for Hassan to be raped. Some may argue that Amir's inaction indirectly resulted in Hassan's and Ali's premature demises since they were separated from Amir and Baba and stayed in Afghanistan. However, it is worth noting that Amir did not want them to die and that he deliberately risked his own life to save Sohrab's.)*

2. Using the Time Line graphic on page 31 of this guide, discuss how the novel correlates with historical events in Afghanistan. In the top boxes, write key dates and a phrase to identify their importance in Afghanistan's history and fill in the bottom boxes with correlating significant events in the lives of the novel's characters. *(1973: Daoud overthrows King Zahir Shah's regime, and Assef threatens Amir and Hassan; 1979–1981: Soviets take control of Afghanistan, and Baba and Amir flee to Pakistan; 1989: The Russians complete their withdrawal from Afghanistan, and Amir's first novel is published; 2001: The Taliban is deposed, and Amir rescues Sohrab and brings him to the United States.)*

3. Using the Cause/Effect Chart on page 32 of this guide, examine (a) Amir's decision to get rid of Hassan and Ali and (b) his decision to save Sohrab. *(a. Cause: Amir's guilt over his betrayal of Hassan; Decision: falsely accuses Hassan of stealing; Result: Ali's and Hassan's departure/Baba's deep sorrow; Result: Amir's mixture of guilt and gladness; b. Cause: Rahim Khan asks Amir to go to Afghanistan and tells him to find Sohrab, who is revealed to be Amir's nephew; Decision: Amir agrees to go; Result: Amir rescues Sohrab and takes him to live with him and Soraya in the United States. Possible Decision: Amir refuses to go; Results: He continues to live with guilt; Assef continues to keep Sohrab as his sex slave; Sohrab commits suicide.)*

4. Using the Characters With Character graphic on page 33 of this guide, assess the traits of various characters in the novel. Note those characters who remain consistent throughout the novel. *(Answers will vary. Tells the truth: Hassan, Ali, Soraya, Sohrab, Rahim Khan and Baba [usually]; Does not: Amir, Baba and Rahim [occasionally], Assef; Keeps promises: Rahim Khan, Hassan, Baba, Amir [eventually], Soraya; Does not: Amir; Considers consequences of actions: Ali, Hassan, Rahim; Does not: Amir, Baba, Sanaubar; Sacrifices for others: Hassan, Ali, Rahim, Baba, Amir [eventually], Farid; Does not: Amir [initially], Assef, Sanaubar; Listens to others without prejudging them: Rahim Khan, Hassan, Soraya; Does not: Baba and Amir [occasionally], Assef, General Taheri; Is a good person: Ali, Hassan, Soraya, Amir and Baba [basically], Rahim Khan, Farid, Sohrab; Is not: Assef, Amir [occasionally], Sanaubar; Is kind and caring: Ali, Hassan, Rahim, Soraya, Amir and Baba [usually], Omar Faisal, Jamila Taheri; Is not: Assef, Sanaubar)*

5. Using the Herringbone Chart on page 34 of this guide, discuss Amir's search for redemption. Use the top three questions to identify what causes his guilt and the bottom three questions to identify how he attempts to find redemption. *(Main Idea: Amir's search for redemption; Where: Kabul, Afghanistan; What: He betrays Hassan by failing to help him when Assef rapes him; He tells no one what happened and falsely accuses Hassan of theft; When: winter and summer of 1975; Who: Rahim Khan offers him a chance to be good again; How: He goes to Kabul and rescues Sohrab; Why: He discovers that Hassan was his half-brother; Assef has taken Sohrab for sexual perversion.)*

6. Using the Story Map on page 35 of this guide, analyze the plot development of the novel. *(Main Characters: Amir, Hassan, Baba, Ali, Rahim Khan, Soraya, Assef, Sohrab; Setting: Afghanistan, Pakistan, United States; 1963–2002; Main Conflict: Amir betrays Hassan and lives with the guilt for 26 years; Summary: [1] Amir and Hassan grow up as constant companions in Kabul; [2] The two boys enter the kite-fighting tournament and win; [3] Assef rapes Hassan when he retrieves the kite for Amir; [4] Amir falsely accuses Hassan of theft, and Ali and Hassan leave Kabul; [5] Baba and Amir flee Afghanistan and go to the United States; [6] Amir marries Soraya, and Baba dies; [7] Rahim Khan calls Amir and offers him a chance to be good again; [8] Amir goes to Peshawar and discovers that Baba also fathered Hassan, and Rahim asks him to rescue Sohrab, who is now an orphan; [9] Amir goes to Kabul and finds Sohrab with Assef; Climax: Assef beats Amir as "payment" for Sohrab, who rescues Amir by shooting Assef with his slingshot; Resolution: Amir takes Sohrab to America to adopt him as his own son.)*

7. Analyze the father/child relationships in the novel. Discuss whether the relationships are static or dynamic. *(Baba/Amir—dynamic: Baba, who is strong and athletic, has trouble accepting Amir, who is mild-mannered and studious. Amir thinks his father hates him because Amir's mother died during his birth. He feels rejected and tries to earn his father's love by winning the kite tournament. Baba feels closer to and more accepting of Amir after they come to America but cannot understand why Amir chooses writing as his profession rather than one that will make him rich. Amir initially feels incapable of surviving without Baba; Ali/Hassan—static: They have a mutual affection and trust. Ali tenderly cares for and guides Hassan and refuses to stay in Baba's service after Amir falsely accuses Hassan of theft; Hassan/Sohrab—static: Their relationship is much like Ali's with Hassan. Hassan sees to it that Sohrab learns to read and write. He is proud of his son. Sohrab loves Hassan and yearns for the life they had before Hassan was killed; General Taheri/Soraya—dynamic: He fulfills the role of a true Afghan father, i.e., protective and strict. When she rebels and runs away with a man to whom she is not married, he goes to get her and forces her to return with him. She initially hates him for this but comes to realize he loves her and wants to save her from destroying her life. He initially does not approve of her choice to become a teacher, but he later attends her classes and takes notes.)*

8. Provide examples of how each of the following themes are developed throughout the novel: guilt/redemption, rejection, discrimination, and friendship. *(guilt/redemption: Soraya's guilt over her indiscretion prompts her to confess to Amir before their marriage, and Amir's love and his knowledge of his own sin resolve the issue. Baba's guilt for fathering Hassan causes him to feel "torn between two halves" [p. 301] of himself, which he deals with by working to better his community. Rahim Khan's guilt over not disclosing the identity of Hassan's father results in Sohrab's rescue. Sanaubar's guilt over deserting Ali and Hassan is resolved when she returns and is received by Hassan with forgiveness and love; rejection: Amir struggles to overcome his father's rejection and finds satisfaction in knowing Baba is proud of him when he graduates from high school and later when Baba acknowledges that he is a good writer; discrimination: The bigotry that causes Pashtuns to discriminate against Hazaras taints the relationship between Baba and Ali and between Amir and Hassan. Hazaras are expected to be subservient and illiterate. This prejudice is largely to blame for Baba's refusal to acknowledge Hassan as his son. Assef is the epitome of bigoted hatred, as illustrated by his reaction to all Hazaras and his desire to see them dead; friendship: Amir's and Hassan's childhood friendship is clouded by Amir's feeling of superiority, yet Hassan tells Sohrab that Amir is the best friend he ever had. As an adult, Amir reflects on the devotion and loyalty of his friend, Hassan. Rahim Khan's friendship helps Amir learn to believe in himself. Baba's Afghan friends show their love and loyalty for him during his illness and after his death.)*

9. One of the novel's main themes is the idea that everything costs something. How does the novel illustrate this? What part do you think people play in determining the ultimate cost of their actions? *(Answers will vary. Baba's affair with Sanaubar costs Ali his honor; The price of the thrill of kite fighting is bloodied fingers; A life spent pursuing pleasure costs Sanaubar many years with her family and her looks; Amir's desire to win Baba's love costs Hassan his sense of dignity; The cost of "peace" under the Taliban's rule is Afghans' personal freedoms and peace of mind; The need to be good again and to show his loyalty to his family and Afghanistan costs Amir the ability to remain ensconced in his successful American life indefinitely; Continued funding for Zaman's orphanage periodically costs orphans their emotional well-being; The cost to save Sohrab from Assef is Amir's physical well-being, etc. As Amir's life illustrates, failing to "pay" a fair moral price for one's actions at an early juncture allows interest to accumulate. Moral problems then compound exponentially.)*

10. What comment does Hosseini mean to make about suffering through this story, and how does Amir come to know that God exists? *(Answers will vary. Hosseini seems to be saying that an imperfect world guarantees suffering, from which no one is exempt. If one realizes that suffering is the natural state of existence, as Hassan does, then one views every good thing that happens as a blessing, not as something owed [as Amir does for much of the novel until he realizes he has taken too much to deserve what he has been given]. Recognizing blessings makes a person grateful, and gratitude nurtures selflessness. Selflessness begets a giving nature, and this we call love. Noted Islamic thinker Dr. Khalid Zaheer suggests that the path to God is love [http://www.renaissance.com.pk/Septq2y5.htm: active at time of publication]. If suffering leads to selflessness, and selflessness leads to the manifesting of love, then it is through suffering that one finds God/a sense of moral responsibility. Amir has this epiphany in the hospital waiting room when so shortly after having been emancipated from the pain of his 26-year-old sin he seems poised to lose Sohrab.)*

11. How might Hosseini say Afghanistan's class system is flawed, and how might Amir's family and their struggles be viewed as a metaphor for Afghanistan's class system? *(One class/race is taught that they are beneath others, and one class/race is taught that treating a certain class/race with the basic human dignity they enjoy is beneath them. In a system such as this, the end result is that neither group of people can hope to actualize their potential as human beings because the system prevents both classes from loving themselves fully. If the path to God is love, then the class system is an obstruction on the path to God. Hate ends up degrading everyone; it just takes longer for the haters to realize that they too are victims. Baba may be viewed as symbolic of Afghanistan. In many ways he is very good and deserving of respect, but the sin of dishonoring one of his own has left him "a man torn between two halves," perpetually conflicted [p. 359]. Amir represents Pashtuns, and Hassan represents Hazaras. Though they come from the same father, his sin has left them unable to realize they are two halves of the same whole. The privileged half's wrongful sense of entitlement causes it to take from the unprivileged half until the resulting social distance between the two leaves them completely isolated from each other. However, by listening to the conscience [Rahim], it is possible for the privileged half to perceive its mirror image in the unprivileged half and mend what is broken.)*

Post-reading Extension Activities

Writing/Speaking

1. Write and present orally a monologue in which Sohrab explains his life before and after coming to America.
2. View the movie version of the novel. Then write a report in which you compare/contrast the two works.
3. Write a sequel set five years after the end of the novel.
4. Using the poem "The Elephant in the Room" by Terry Kettering as a model (Source: http://www.geocities.com/tcf-troy/OthersWrite/ElephantInRoom.html?200812; active at time of publication), write a poem about an "elephant in the room" from the novel, e.g., Rahim Khan's illness, Baba's illness and/or death, Amir's guilt, or Amir and Soraya's inability to have a child. Then read your poem to the class.

Drama/Music

5. Working with a small group, write and stage a different ending for the novel.
6. Write and perform a ballad telling the love story of Amir and Soraya.
7. Working with a small group, stage a scene from the novel. Add appropriate background music and lighting.

Art

8. Create a collage depicting Amir's guilt and his search for redemption.
9. Prepare a montage showing the devastation various political regimes caused in Afghanistan.
10. Design a poster advertising the novel.

Research/Current Events

11. Bring to class current newspaper and magazine articles relating to the ongoing strife in Afghanistan. Display these on a poster board with appropriate headings.
12. Research and write a report about Afghanistan's current political leaders.

Assessment for *The Kite Runner*

Assessment is an ongoing process. The following ten items can be completed during study of the novel. Once finished, the student and teacher will check the work. Points may be added to indicate the level of understanding.

Name _____ Date _____

Student **Teacher**

_____ _____ 1. Keep a literary journal from Amir's perspective as you read the book.

_____ _____ 2. Using at least ten vocabulary words, write a summary of the novel.

_____ _____ 3. Write three review questions, and use these to participate in an oral review.

_____ _____ 4. Play the "Vocabulary Wheel" game on page 36 of this guide.

_____ _____ 5. Write a riddle about a character in the novel. Exchange riddles with a partner, and identify each other's character. Read the riddle and your response aloud to the class.

_____ _____ 6. Correct all quizzes taken over the course of the novel.

_____ _____ 7. Share your Post-reading Extension Activity with the class on the assigned day.

_____ _____ 8. Working in a small group, share your completed vocabulary, comprehension, character analysis, and literary analysis activities.

_____ _____ 9. Write a review of the novel for your school newspaper.

_____ _____ 10. Choose a theme from the novel, and explain to the class how it is developed, e.g., the divisive effects of discrimination, the pain of rejection, the transformative power of guilt, the search for redemption, the importance of family and loyalty.

Metaphors and Similes

A **metaphor** is a comparison between two unlike objects. For example, "he was a human tree." A **simile** is a comparison between two unlike objects that uses the words *like* or *as*. For example, "the color of her eyes was like the cloudless sky."

Directions: Complete the chart below by listing metaphors and similes from the novel, as well as the page numbers on which they are found. Identify metaphors with an "M" and similes with an "S." Translate the comparisons in your own words, and then list the objects being compared.

Metaphors/Similes	Ideas/Objects Being Compared
1. Translation:	
2. Translation:	
3. Translation:	

Time Line

Directions: In the top boxes, write key dates and a phrase to identify important events in Afghanistan's history. Fill in the bottom boxes with correlating significant events in the lives of the novel's characters.

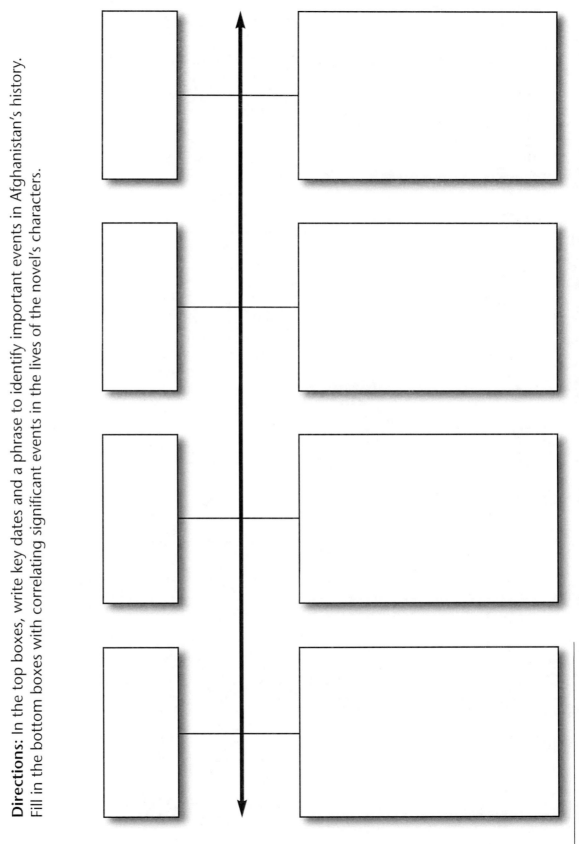

Cause/Effect Chart

Directions: In the first chart, examine Amir's decision to get rid of Hassan and Ali. In the second chart, examine Amir's decision to save Sohrab.

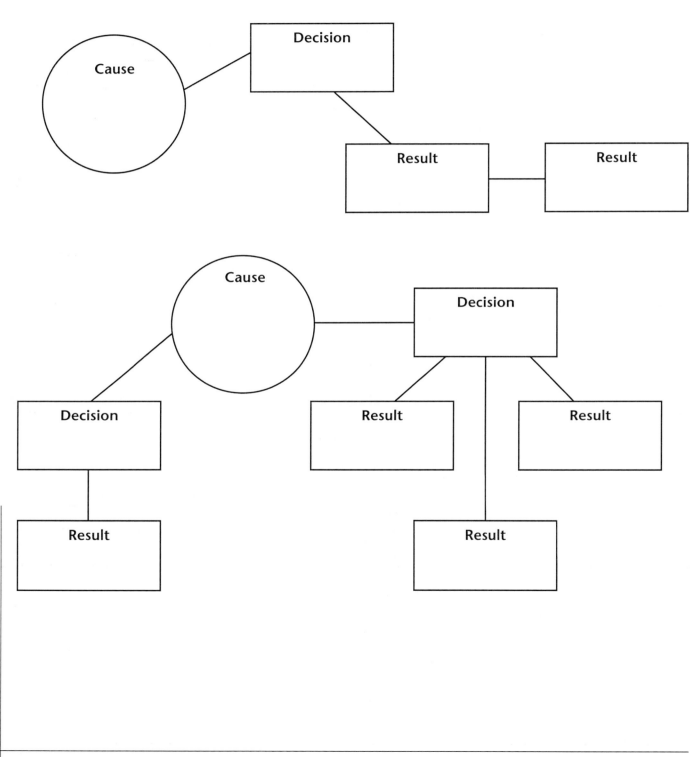

Characters With Character

Directions: A person's **character** is evaluated by his or her actions, statements, and by the way he or she treats others. For each of the attributes listed in the center of the page, write the name of one character from the novel who has this trait and the name of a character who does **not** have this trait. After each character's name, give an example of an action or statement which proves you have properly evaluated the character.

Has This Trait		Doesn't Have This Trait
	tells the truth	
	keeps promises	
	considers consequences of actions	
	sacrifices for others	
	listens to others without pre-judging them	
	is a good person	
	is kind and caring	

Herringbone Chart

Directions: Use the diagram to examine Amir's search for redemption. Use the top three questions to identify what causes his guilt and the bottom three questions to identify how he attempts to find redemption.

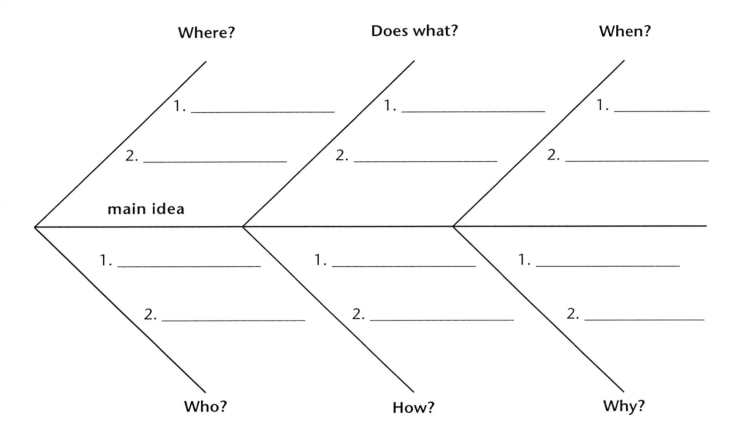

Story Map

Directions: Fill in each box below with information about the novel.

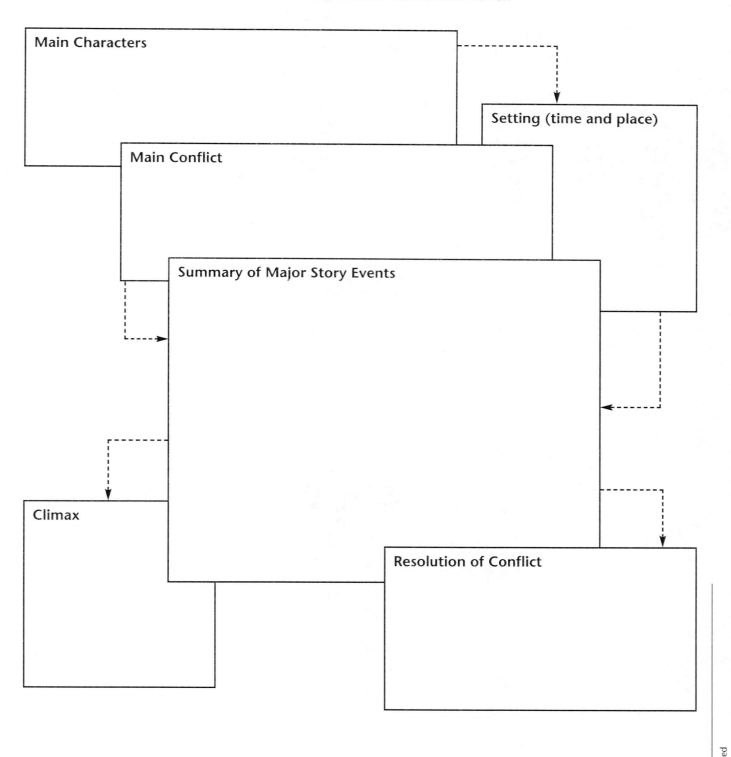

Vocabulary Wheel

Directions: Write each vocabulary word on a piece of paper (one word per piece). Make a spinner using the circle below. Now play the following game with a classmate. (It is a good idea to have a dictionary and thesaurus handy.) Place the papers in a small container. The first player draws a word from the container. The player then spins the spinner and follows the direction where the pointer lands. For example, if the player draws the word "trolley" and lands on "Define," the player must define the word trolley. If the player's partner accepts the answer as correct, the first player scores one point and play passes to the second player. If the player's partner challenges the answer, the first player uses a dictionary or thesaurus to prove the answer is correct. If the player can prove the answer is correct, the player earns two points. If the player cannot prove the answer is correct, the opposing player earns two points. Play continues until all the words have been used. The player with the most points wins.

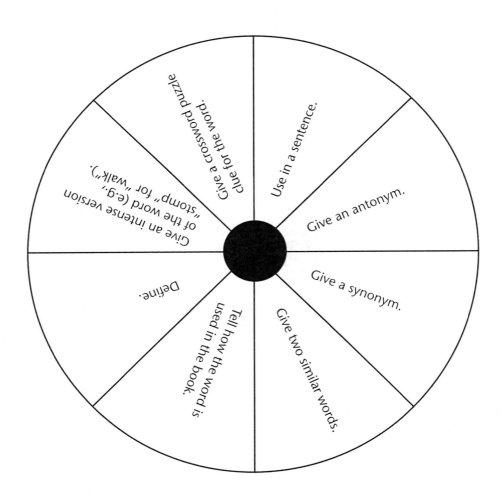

Linking Novel Units® Lessons to National and State Reading Assessments

During the past several years, an increasing number of students have faced some form of state-mandated competency testing in reading. Many states now administer state-developed assessments to measure the skills and knowledge emphasized in their particular reading curriculum. The discussion questions and post-reading questions in this Novel Units® Teacher Guide make excellent open-ended comprehension questions and may be used throughout the daily lessons as practice activities. The rubric below provides important information for evaluating responses to open-ended comprehension questions. Teachers may also use scoring rubrics provided for their own state's competency test.

Please note: The Novel Units® Student Packet contains optional open-ended questions in a format similar to many national and state reading assessments.

Scoring Rubric for Open-Ended Items

3-Exemplary
- Thorough, complete ideas/information
- Clear organization throughout
- Logical reasoning/conclusions
- Thorough understanding of reading task
- Accurate, complete response

2-Sufficient
- Many relevant ideas/pieces of information
- Clear organization throughout most of response
- Minor problems in logical reasoning/conclusions
- General understanding of reading task
- Generally accurate and complete response

1-Partially Sufficient
- Minimally relevant ideas/information
- Obvious gaps in organization
- Obvious problems in logical reasoning/conclusions
- Minimal understanding of reading task
- Inaccuracies/incomplete response

0-Insufficient
- Irrelevant ideas/information
- No coherent organization
- Major problems in logical reasoning/conclusions
- Little or no understanding of reading task
- Generally inaccurate/incomplete response

Glossary

Chapters One–Four

1. unatoned: not having made amends for
2. cleft lip: harelip; a deformity existing from birth in which parts of the upper lip fail to grow together
3. ethnic: having to do with racial and cultural groups of people
4. Mongoloid: a race that is characterized as having yellowish skin, slanting eyes, prominent cheekbones, a short, broad nose, and straight, dark hair
5. mullah: a teacher of the sacred law of the Koran
6. aficionados: devotees; fans
7. impeccable: faultless; irreproachable; not to be doubted
8. imbecile: a person who never develops beyond the mental age of eight
9. hone: sharpen; develop
10. irony: when the actual result of a sequence of events is the opposite of the normal or expected result

Chapters Five–Seven

1. coup d'état: a sudden and decisive act in politics that usually produces a change of government by force
2. monarchy: a government in which a single person has the power to rule
3. republic: a nation in which the citizens elect representatives to manage the government, which is usually headed by a president
4. sociopath: a person who is interested only in his/her personal needs and desires, without concern for the effects of his/her behavior on others
5. hierarchy: a system in which persons are arranged into higher and lower ranks or classes
6. nuances: shades of expressions or meanings
7. integrity: honesty; sincerity; uprightness
8. viable: workable; that which can be put to use
9. morose: moody; sullen; ill-humored
10. sallow: having a sickly, yellowish color
11. beneficent: doing good; kind
12. guileless: without deceit; honest

Chapters Eight–Ten

1. unkempt: neglected; untidy; not cared for
2. insomniac: a person who suffers from the inability to sleep
3. periphery: outside boundary
4. pregnant: filled; loaded

5. alter ego: another aspect of a person's own nature
6. mortal: deadly; fatal
7. bile: a bitter, greenish-yellow liquid secreted by the liver; aids digestion
8. lucrative: profitable; productive
9. elopement: the act of escaping by running away
10. rueful: apologetic; remorseful
11. encapsulated: enclosed in a protective covering

Chapters Eleven–Thirteen

1. de facto: in fact; in reality
2. cretin: stupid person
3. acrid: sharp; bitter; pungent
4. coyly: shyly; reservedly
5. tenets: doctrines; principles; beliefs
6. chastity: moral purity; virtue
7. kiosk: small structure with one or more sides open
8. pulmonary: of or having to do with the lungs
9. pathology: a brand of medicine that studies the causes and nature of diseases
10. palliative: something that lessens or softens pain or disease
11. oncologist: a person who studies and treats cancerous tumors
12. mosque: a place of public worship for Muslims
13. chagrin: feeling of disappointment, failure, or humiliation
14. overt: open; evident; not hidden
15. ambivalent: having or showing conflicting attitudes or feelings

Chapters Fourteen–Nineteen

1. soliloquies: speeches in which a person talks to himself
2. garrulous: talking too much; long-winded
3. collateral damage: killing of civilians or damaging of nonmilitary structures in the course of military operations such as a bombing raid
4. melancholic: gloomy; emotionally depressed
5. pragmatic: viewing things in a practical, matter-of-fact way
6. affable: friendly; genial; courteous and respectful of others
7. empathy: the process of mentally entering fully into another's feelings or motives; compassion
8. snickered: laughing in a half-repressed, disrespectful way
9. jihad: religious war of Muslims against nonbelievers

10. cursory: hasty; superficial
11. impregnated: filled with; saturated

Chapters Twenty–Twenty-Two
1. unadulterated: pure; unmodified
2. gingerly: with extreme care or caution; warily
3. mosaic: picture or design made up of small pieces or images
4. cleric: clergyman
5. sanctity: holiness; sacredness
6. Mecca: birthplace of Mohammed and holiest city of Islam, located in Saudi Arabia
7. guru: spiritual leader or guide
8. furtive: secretive; cautious
9. surreal: dreamlike distortion of reality
10. epiphany: a sudden revelation or perception
11. bourgeoisie: persons of the middle class

Chapters Twenty-Three–Twenty-Four
1. pneumothorax: the presence of air in the chest cavity
2. impunity: freedom from punishment or other bad consequences
3. squalid: very dirty; filthy
4. harried: stressed; anxious; agitated
5. milieu: surroundings; environment
6. asylum: refuge; shelter; sanctuary
7. nimbus: a luminous vapor, cloud, or atmosphere
8. humanitarian visa: official endorsement that allows a person who is in dire need to enter a country

Chapter Twenty-Five
1. benevolent: generous; compassionate; desiring to help others
2. serpentine: twisting; winding
3. protocol: rules for any procedure
4. myriad: a very great number
5. catharsis: an emotional purification or relief
6. eccentric: out of the ordinary; odd; unconventional
7. melee: noisy, confused tumult